# PUDSEY
## & DISTRICT

DONALD EKE, EVA MILNER,
EUNICE TONGE

The
History
Press

John Lee, fish and
rabbit salesman,
pre-1914.

First published in 1995
Reprinted in 2000
This edition first published in 2009

The History Press
The Mill, Brimscombe Port
Stroud, Gloucestershire, GL5 2QG
www.thehistorypress.co.uk

British Library Cataloguing in Publication Data.
A catalogue record for this book is available from the British Library.

ISBN: 978 0 7524 5317 0

Typesetting and origination by The History Press
Printed in Great Britain

# CONTENTS

BE JUST AND FEAR NOT

PUDSEY.

REG?
TRADE MARK.

HERALDIC SERIES.

Pudsey coat of arms, described in the introduction.

# INTRODUCTION

This collection of photographs is a record of three places, Pudsey, Farsley and Calverley, which were separate settlements from before the Norman Conquest until 1937, when they were amalgamated to form the Borough of Pudsey. In 1974 this was absorbed into Leeds Metropolitan District. The coat of arms shows four shuttles and a woolsack, indicating Pudsey's dependence on wool. The grant of the coat of arms was made in 1901, and the civic mace and amorial bearings were presented by public subscription. The motto, in English, is 'Be Just and Fear Not'.

In the eleventh century Pudsey was owned by two Saxon thanes, Dunstan and Stainulf, who also owned estates in other parts of Yorkshire. After the Conquest Pudsey became the possession of Ilbert de Lacy, who later became Baron of Pontefract. The Domesday Book states: 'In Pudsey Dunstan and Stainulf had eight caracutes of land, where there might be four ploughs. Ilbert has it, and it is waste. Value in King Edward's time, forty shillings.' At the same time, Farsley and Calverley were each valued at twenty shillings.

During the following centuries Pudsey depended largely on farming and sheep-rearing, the fleeces being woven on hand-looms in the cottages. By the late eighteenth century there were small scribbling (the early stage of spinning woollen yarn) mills, at first using horse power but later steam power. When woven the cloth was taken to water powered fulling mills to give the required felt finish. There were fulling mills at Calverley Bridge, Shipley, Esholt and Harewood. In this district the woollen cloth was woven on handlooms until the 1860s.

The nineteenth century brought steam power and the building of much larger mills, and a great expansion of trade. The steam-powered mills were used for spinning and fulling only, the weaving still continuing on hand-looms. Ancillary trades of leatherworking, tannery, dyeing, glue and size making were established. In Pudsey and nearby Stanningley, textile engineering and later railway engineering were introduced. Quarrying was carried on and there were several small coalpits.

Recently the textile industry has virtually disappeared. Many mills have been leased out to light industry, or pulled down to make way for housing.

In this collection of nearly 200 photographs we see many aspects of life in Pudsey in the last 100 years. Many crowded streets and folds have disappeared – not always a matter of regret, as many of them must have been dark and dirty. Several of the large imposing chapels have been demolished or have been converted to other uses. The Pudseyites were not perhaps so religious as their numerous chapels would seem to indicate. Much of the social and recreational life of the town was bound up with chapel and church, with cricket and football teams, socials, bazaars, garden parties, processions and open-air hymn singing. If you didn't belong to a chapel or church, you were not one of the 'in-crowd'.

We hope that many happy memories will be stirred by these photographs, and that those who are too young to remember may be interested to find out how people used to live in Pudsey in days gone by.

The compilers have tried to be accurate, but if any errors have crept in it would be appreciated if these are pointed out.

Donald Eke
Eva Milner
Eunice Tonge
September 1995

A bonfire at Pudsey on the recreation ground, Calverley Lane. It was built for the coronation of King George V in 1911.

# Section One

# ROUND ABOUT PUDSEY

*Church Lane, looking east. On the left is the entrance to the Wesleyan chapel.*

Chapeltown with war memorial. The vicar of Pudsey parish church, the Revd John Vipond, leads a Remembrance Day service in 1962. The memorial was unveiled on Sunday 10 September 1922 by the mayor, E.J. Byrd. The pedestal is of granite and is surmounted by a bronze figure of a soldier of the West Yorkshire Regiment, 8 ft in height. The wreaths and tablets for names are also bronze. The memorial occupies the site of the former chapel-of-ease, which was demolished in 1879 after becoming dilapidated.

Lowtown, looking west, *c.* 1900. This view shows the junction of Lowtown and Manor House Street. The Co-op store is on the left and in the distance Druggist's Corner stands where the present traffic lights are.

Lowtown, looking east, *c.* 1900. The frontage of the well-known grocer's shop, James C. Booth, appears on the left, at the corner of Booth's Yard.

Booth's Yard, Lowtown. This group of buildings is mainly of late seventeenth-century date, and was formerly called Hammerton Fold. They were in a very run-down state until bought by Mr Prideaux for restoration in about 1981. The remains of medieval workshops and buildings were uncovered by a group of volunteers led by Mr Andrew McDermid. The photograph shows the restored buildings, now occupied by a variety of small businesses and shops.

Waver Green is the original site of the market, at the junction of Robin Lane and Church Lane. The small buildings include Job Wilcock's hot pea saloon and 'Tripey' Ross's shop.

The Manor House occupied the site in Robin Lane, opposite the end of Manor House Street. Mostly of seventeenth-century construction, it was formerly the home of the Milner family. It was converted into business use, and demolished eventually in 1910.

A view from Owlcoates, looking towards Ilkley Moor, shows in the foreground the cricket field of the Pudsey Unitarian Cricket Club. The hut is the cricket pavilion. The roller can be seen against the hedge, to the right. Beyond the haystacks is the GNR (Great Northern Railway, part of the later LNER). Behind the chimney on the left, belonging to the Leeds and Bradford Boiler Company, is a large field, Cotefield. Priesthorpe Farm is above the middle telegraph pole. Priesthorpe Lane and Cote Lane were then country lanes, famous for blackberries. After the war, in 1945, a large council estate was built on Cotefield and the adjoining Farfield.

Lidget Hill, *c.* 1910. Although there is a tram in the picture, there appears to be little fear of other traffic. On the left is a wooden hut owned by Mrs Ross of the tripe-dressing family. All the property on the left has been replaced by two-storey shops and offices.

Radcliffe Lane, about 1830. The newly built church stands out at the top of the hill. Radcliffe Lane was then bordered by farms and fields.

Parish church and park, 1904. The swans were a popular feature of the park when this picture was taken, and the swan-house is on the right. The lake was superseded in 1935 by a Jubilee Garden, which was created to commemorate the Silver Jubilee of King George V and Queen Mary.

*Opposite*: The Pudsey Pudding cartoon was drawn to commemorate a unique event in Pudsey's history. To celebrate the repeal of the Corn Laws, in 1846, a 'monster plum pudding' was made. Twenty housewives mixed one stone of flour each, with fruit and suet in proportion. The mixture was boiled for three days and nights in a specially scoured-out dyepan at Crawshaw Mills. The pudding was paraded round the streets in a wherry, adorned with flags and banners, to the delight of the watching crowds. On 31 July 1846 the pudding was divided into 1s portions, the recipients supplying fork or spoon. The paying customers ate first, seated at trestle tables in a field next to the mill. When all were satisfied, the 'hungry onlookers' were allowed to finish off the last of Pudsey's monster plum pudding. In 1878, Mr W.D. Scales, boot and shoe manufacturer, of Grove House, had a window made for his home, using the cartoon as a pattern. It was for many years a feature of the billiard-room, but unfortunately it has not survived.

Enthusiastic children show off their prowess on the climbing frame in Pudsey park, *c.* 1960.

The drinking fountain in the park was given to the town by Mr W.D. Scales in 1889, when the park was opened. The tablet on the fountain reads: 'This fountain was erected and dedicated to the public by W.D. Scales, 1889.' In view of his well-known temperance convictions, this was an appropriate gift.

This floral display was designed and planted by the Parks Department to commemorate sixty years of scouting in Pudsey in 1967. Admiring the blooms are Scout Commissioner Eric Goodair, and Mayor George Dunkerley.

The first shelter in the park, 1895. The park was opened in 1889 at a cost of £4,750. In the background is the Park Hotel dating from 1734, although it did not become an inn until the 1820s.

The children's playground in the park occupies part of the former recreation ground of the town. The equipment was given to Pudsey by Councillor John B. Ward, and opened in 1928.

## Section Two

# WORK AND SHOPPING

*J. Nicholson, decorator, setting off for a job with his horse and van, c. 1900.*

Frank Parkinson's pig farm, 1927. The farm occupied the site of the present-day Fartown Close. The young boy is Frank's son Norman, who was a gifted musician. He played the cornet and also sang in the parish church choir.

W. Davey, the baker, delivering bread in Somerset Road, 1910. The houses in the background are externally very much the same today.

The exterior of Samuel Wade's Excelsior Laundry, Occupation Lane. Before the advent of washing-machines, the vans would be kept busy delivering laundry to the bigger houses in Pudsey.

Interior view of the laundry. White collars are much in evidence in this scene. A clean well-starched collar was the hallmark of respectability at the turn of the century. The women are using gas irons, which were a recent invention; most people used flat irons heated on the fire.

The Royal Cinema, Bradford Road, was constructed of brick and corrugated iron, and was known locally as the 'Tin Trunk'. A licence was granted to the Royal, under the Cinematograph Act 1909, as early as March 1911. Former patrons remember the whole building rumbling when a train passed on the line behind, completely ruining a tense scene in a Western or gangster film.

Pictured outside his shop in Richardshaw Lane is J.W. Nield, fish and rabbit salesman, 1906. The child on the cart later became Councillor Nield.

Leigh Mills, Stanningley. In 1896 the Leigh Mills Company leased works at Stanningley and installed spinning and weaving machinery. In 1918 a new spinning mill was built on nearby land for worsted yarn. At its peak production, the firm had 400 looms and employed 1,000 workers.

This typical small shop was run by the Entwistle family in Bradford Road, c. 1930. The two women are Jane Entwistle and Evelyn Smithson, née Entwistle.

A group of workers at Stanningley station, 1916. During the war women took on traditional men's jobs, and we see here a woman in railway uniform. The man on the front row (third from left) is wearing clogs, the usual footwear for workmen of the time.

OLD MILL AND BRID
RODLEY

The last textile mill at Calverley Bridge. Records show a mill on this site in the fourteenth century, though it was then a corn mill. Later it became a fulling mill, but now it is demolished.

Mary Moorhouse's shop, Delph End, 1900. This shop served the cottages which sprang up around Gibraltar Mill. At this time it stocked groceries, beer and porter; it appears that hats, ornaments and pictures were also on sale.

Outside the Leeds Industrial Co-operative Society's shop in Greenside, 1927. The manager, Johnny Pearson, and employees John Stanley, Turner Johnson, George Leffley and Joe Whiteley are shown.

Peel's confectioners and sweet shop, Littlemoor Road, *c.* 1930. The names of the women are not known.

Customers wait their turn to be served at the counter of Jesse Stephenson's store in Chapeltown, Pudsey. It was one of fifty-three branches opened since the first one was established in Town Street, Farsley, in 1903. The family also owned the Sunshine Bakery and warehouse, New Street, and in the company's heyday there were about fifty delivery vans taking bread and provisions to the branches daily.

Two unusual shops are shown here. They are part of the structure of the Picture House, Church Lane, Pudsey. Patrons could buy their sweets and tobacco from W. Rogers' shop as they entered the cinema, the shop on the other side of the entrance being a ladies' fashion shop owned by a husband-and-wife team, A. and G. Crossley. The cinema was later converted into a supermarket, and the two shops were pulled down to allow for pavement-widening. Pudsey's other cinema, the Palace, has also been converted to other uses.

# Section Three

# SPORT AND LEISURE

*This photograph is believed to be of Pudsey Britannia Cricket Club, c. 1900.*

*Unfortunately, none of the names are known.*

A crowd of spectators watches the riders in the Motorcycle Hill Climb Trials in the 1920s, when this was a popular sport. The venue is Post Hill.

The Pudsey Congregational Sunday School Football Club, 1922. Back row, left to right: E. Jackson, R. Summersgill, M. Gambles, E. Kaye, L. Scott, J. Tidgewell. Middle row: F. Moss, W. Sowden, H. Brayshaw, N. Pitts, A. Scott. Front row: L. Ramsden, L. Sutcliffe, D.B. Wilson, W.V. Walker, W. Lewis.

Stanningley Congregational Church billards team, 1926. Back row, left to right: S. Midgeley, W. Kaye, A. Moorhouse. Front row: G. Wood, J. Carter, H. Hunt.

The football team of W.C. Forrest are the victors in the Pudsey Town AFC Inter-works competition, 1928. Back row, left to right: are E. Pawson (trainer), J.W. Simpson, H. Gaunt, C. Scott, L. Armitage, W. Raistrick, H. Burton (secretary). Middle row: H. Gillingwater, L. Howe, H. Unwin, J. Moss, E. Whittaker. Front row: G. Wood (captain).

Pudsey Britannia Cricket Club, 1930. Among the team members are W. Waters, 'Lobby' Armitage, Jack Rider, Firth Moorhouse, John Willie Simpson and J. Hartley.

Alderman Clark, mayor of Pudsey in 1954, is showing the lucky coin used for the toss in test matches by Len Hutton (far right). Miss J. Clark, mayoress, Mr R. Cruse, town clerk, and Mrs V. Cruse look on.

The distinguished Yorkshire and England captain, Len Hutton, goes out to bat on 3 August 1938 at the Oval, where he created a world record of 364 runs against the Australians in the test match. He was born and brought up in Fulneck.

St John's Ambulance Cadets receive their Grand Prior badges, 1954. Back row, left to right: Margaret Kendall, M. Hayes, Dorothy Ramsden, Joan Fowler, Muriel Shipman, Lily Davies. Front row: Elsie Walker (Cadet Superintendent), Joan Davies, Nurse Rawcliffe, Mary Laister and Mary Page (Cadet Officer).

Members of the Pudsey Group Scouts enjoy the fun at their bazaar, December 1959. Among those pictured here are Stewart Tyson, Phillip Tyson, John Tyson, Tim Shaw, Paul Depledge, Brian Parkinson.

The Old Grammarians Hockey XI, 1957. They are former pupils of Pudsey Grammar School. Back row, left to right: Margaret Grimshaw, Shirley Hainsworth, Wendy Jamieson, Marjorie Nichols, Margaret Jamieson, Mollie Illingworth. Front row: Peggy O'Neill, Jean Threapleton, Ina Wilkinson (captain), Jacqui Harris, Joan Hopps.

The Pudsey Rotary and Round Table Ladies' Cricket Team ready for action, 1961.

Linda Gordon, of 1st Pudsey Guides, receives the Queen's Guide award, 1964.

A smiling president and guests enjoy the Fulneck Golf Club dinner, 1966. Left to right: Mr M.L. Rowe (president, East Bierley Golf Club), Mr A. Gaunt (Fulneck captain), Mr E. Wilson (Fulneck president), Mr L. Metcalfe (president, Bradford Union Golf Clubs), and Mr L. Ramsden (Fulneck Golf Club).

These are the members of the Ladies keep-fit class in Pudsey, 1966. They include Barbara Faulkner, Gwen Langley, Dorothy Dale, Margaret Atkinson, Alma Escrit, Ann Springthorp, Ivy Dutson, Iris Wood, Margaret Johnson, Rose Hirst, Corinne Lazenby, Jean Hall, Jean Booth, Bessie Bentley, Dorothy Herring and Doreen Rothery.

Members of the 2nd Leeds (Pudsey) Boys' Brigade show their trophies, 27 April 1967.

All these cups and awards were won by Pudsey ice skater Phyllida Beck between 1964 and 1971, when the picture was taken.

The Littlemoor Working Men's bowls team show the Bowls Challenge Shield which they won in 1966. Back row, left to right: L. Cox, G. Hitchcock, D. Holdsworth, T. Durrans, P. Watson, H. Sanderson, F. Sanderson. Front row: A. Wilcock, S. Burniston, G. Hobbs, W. Tomlinson, G. Geldart, B. Rayner, S. Geldart.

These Brownies of the 3rd Pudsey Brownie Pack are celebrating the twenty-first anniversary of their formation, 1967. The girls are Gillian Fox, Helen Banks, Carol Banks, Julie Mitchell, with Guiders Miss C. Hare (District Secretary), Mrs A. Lumby, Miss M. Grunwell (Brown Owl), Mrs J.R.B. Turner (Divisional Commissioners), and Miss S.M. Longbottom (District Commissioner).

The trophy for the most life-saving awards was presented to these members of the Pudsey Swimming Club at their annual gala in 1964.

Ronnie Clifford, boxer, receives congratulations from Alderman Harry Keighley, mayor of Pudsey, at the Fulneck Sports and Athletic Club, 1961.

The three winners in the Junior Breast Stroke Race at Pudsey Swimming Club annual gala, 1971. Left to right: Elizabeth Nelson (second), Katrina Dunne (first), and Louise Hazell (third).

Members of Farsley Art Club submit their work to a 'Hit or Miss' panel of judges, with chairman Mike Gill to keep order, 1967.

Pudsey Boys' Brigade drummers and band lead a procession down Carlisle Road, probably for a Remembrance Day service.

# *Section Four*

# CHURCHES AND CHAPELS

*Pudsey parish church from the park, 1924. This view shows the buttresses which*
*extend beyond the roofline on the upper and lower roofs, forming pinnacles.*

The Diamond Jubilee souvenir postcard, commemorating the growth of Richardshaw Lane Primitive Methodist Church, was issued in 1925. The first chapel and school were opened in cottages in 1835 and 1856. Larger premises were soon needed, and a second chapel was opened in 1865, and a new school in 1908.

Sunfield Wesleyan Methodist Chapel, Stanningley, opened for worship in 1839. The cost of the stone and hewing work for the front was borne by Joseph Winn of Newlay Quarries, while the pillars and ironwork were donated by John Butler of Stanningley Ironworks. The chapel has now been demolished.

This interior view of Mount Zion Methodist Church shows it decorated for Christmas services by Mr Packer, in 1966.

After many years of meeting in converted barns and members' houses, the Dissenters built a small chapel in 1708, in Chapeltown, on land formerly occupied by an ox-barn. This chapel was superseded by the one pictured, which had its own graveyard. It opened in 1794.

This handsome Congregational church was opened in Chapeltown in 1866. The building cost £3,059, of which more than £2,000 was raised by subscriptions and collections. It was demolished in 1976, the site now being occupied by housing for the elderly.

Chapeltown, *c.* 1900. The spire of the Congregational church can be seen on the skyline. The Conservative Club is on the right in the foreground, next to Jones the grocers.

At the opening ceremony of the Church Homes, Tofts Road, in July 1923, are Dr Perowne, Bishop of Bradford, and the vicar of Pudsey parish church, the Revd Owen French, in cloak and top hat.

A well-dressed crowd, including many children, at the opening of the Baptist Sunday School Primary Department, in Littlemoor Road, 1898. This building was opened as a Baptist chapel in 1851, but it soon became inadequate and a larger chapel was built on adjoining land. This opened in 1897, and the original chapel was taken over as a Sunday school, evidently a very popular one.

The young men are holding aloft the banner of the Pudsey Baptist Sunday School before setting off on the Whit Monday walk in 1913. Behind can be seen a queue of people who will follow the banner. Whit Monday was a very important day of celebration for all denominations, with processions from each church and chapel. Many of the parades had bands; Mount Tabor even took their harmonium with them on a cart on at least one occasion. Everyone sang hymns before an afternoon of children's sports, followed by tea and currant buns. Simeon Rayner's *History of Pudsey*, published in 1887, gives some idea of the numbers involved. The Whit Monday walk in 1886 drew the following numbers: parish church, 778; St Paul's, 230; Fulneck, 334; Congregationalists, 420; United Methodist Free Church, 793; Primitive Methodists, 813; Mount Zion, 256; Baptists, 110; Wesleyan Methodists, 650; Unitarians, 150; Bethel, 134. The total number of teachers and Sunday school scholars was 4,668.

The Old Clock Chapel, Lowtown, was erected in 1816 for the Methodists. The first preaching house, which had opened in 1773 opposite the present Manor Hall, soon became too small. The Methodists supported two Sunday schools, one at the top and the other at the bottom of Lowtown.

The Trinity Methodist Chapel, Lowtown, was built on the site of the Clock Chapel, and opened on 1 May 1899. It ceased to be used as a church in 1982 and has been converted into an arts centre and shopping mall, while keeping the exterior intact.

The Wesleyan Chapel, Church Lane, was opened in June 1892. It had accommodation for 600 persons and cost £2,000. It has now been demolished to make way for the DHSS building.

An interior view of the Trinity Methodist Chapel, showing the large raised pulpit and the upper galleries 1904. The organ was presented by Thomas Lund: the pipes are arranged on either side of the choir gallery with the console in the centre. This chapel soon developed a fine choral tradition. The large window was donated to the chapel by Squire Spencer, as a memorial to his parents.

St Paul's Church, Stanningley, was built in 1853 in the Old English style. The building is no longer used as a church but has been adapted for business use, and the dedication incorporated into that of the parish church, which is now known as St Lawrence and St Paul.

A procession of parishioners, headed by the choir, sets off from St Paul's church on 28 May 1964.

# Section Five

# TRANSPORT AND ENGINEERING

*A diesel multiple unit at Lowtown station, the day before closure, 1964.*

Pudsey Greenside station was opened in 1878 in response to public pressure, and had a large goods yard to serve the local mills. The line was extended in 1893 to rejoin the main line at Laisterdyke, which entailed the construction of a long tunnel at Smalewell and a massive embankment across the valley of Pudsey Beck. When this picture was taken, in 1897, there were sixty passenger trains a day calling at Greenside station. The opening of the new line facilitated a circular train service from Leeds Central via Pudsey, Dudley Hill, Low Moor, Thornhill, Dewsbury, Batley and Tingley in both directions. The journey time was eighty to ninety minutes for a journey of 29¾ miles.

As a contrast, this photograph shows the last train leaving Greenside station on the evening of 18 June 1964. In the distance can be seen the Royal Hotel, Carlisle Road bridge and the entrance to the tunnel.

A group of people on Stanningley station, c. 1900. The GNR Ivatt D2 class 4–4–0 locomotive is approaching the platform. It was allocated to Leeds engine shed from 1899 to 1912, and remained in service until August 1948.

A view of the entrance to Stanningley station. Hansom cabs and hackney carriages wait for passengers.
The railway serving Stanningley was the Leeds, Bradford and Halifax Junction railway, opened on 31 July
1854. It amalgamated with the GNR in 1865. The man with the shovel and clay pipe probably worked in
the coalyard, part of which can be seen on the right. The stone wall surrounds the coal drops, which
allowed coal to be unloaded into bunkers from the bottom doors of wagons.

Calverley and Rodley station was on the first line into Bradford built by the Leeds and Bradford Railway Company. It opened on 1 July 1846, and was closed on 22 March 1965.

The first tram to Pudsey. Trams had run from Leeds to Stanningley from 1902, until, on 5 June 1908, the line was extended via Richardshaw Lane, Market Place and Chapeltown. The first tram is at Druggist's Corner, with Mayor Joseph Huggan at the controls.

This train, travelling at speed through Stanningley station in about 1900, is a Manchester or Liverpool express of the Lancashire & Yorkshire Railway, headed by an Aspinall 4–4–2 'Atlantic' locomotive. Above the plume of steam from the engine can be seen a GNR centre-pivoted 'somersault' signal, which were introduced on the GNR following a serious accident at Abbots Ripton in January 1876, when the signal arms became frozen to the posts. The number of wagons in the yard shows how busy the railways were when they were the main carriers. Behind the fence, the derrick and railway wagons are in the permanent way maintenance yard, established by the Leeds, Bradford & Halifax Junction Railway in 1854 and still in use today, although special road/rail vehicles are used. In the background with its smoking chimney is Isaac Gaunt's Grangefield Mill, built in 1871. This mill had its own siding, and Isaac Gaunt had his own railway wagons for bringing coal to the mill.

Compartment boats were introduced by the Aire and Calder Navigation in 1864, to compete with the railway transport. This boat was made by Stanningley Ironworks in about 1900. Each of the boats, nicknamed 'Tom Puddings', could carry up to 40 tons of coal to Goole docks, and trains of up to twenty boats were pulled by steam tugs. The tonnage carried rose between 1890 and 1913, from 1 million tons to 3 million tons per year. This method of transporting coal ceased in 1986.

This 256 ft span for the Langar River Bridge was made in 1914 inside the Stanningley Ironworks. Afterwards it was dismantled and loaded on to several trains for the first stage of its long journey to the Federated Malay States.

This example of a railway wagon, from Butler's catalogue, is typical of the type of wagon made at Stanningley Ironworks. In the late nineteenth century, Butler's of Stanningley employed about a thousand men.

Site of the former Stanningley Ironworks, established by Joseph Butler, a moulder from Low Moor, Bradford, in 1828. Under John Butler, son of the founder, they became manufacturers of structural ironwork and railway equipment. The cast-iron girders for Gauxholme Viaduct at Todmorden were made by Butler's in 1840, and are still in use today. The branch line, which can be seen crossing Stanningley Town Street, was built in 1853 after an application to the Leeds, Bradford & Halifax Junction Railway Board. The office building seen in the photograph was unusual in that it completely enclosed the Old Foundry pub, which served the workers in the ironworks. The entrance was through a doorway, now blocked, below the number 600. Although the Butlers became bankrupt in 1896, the works continued in their name until the site was taken over by George Cohen in 1930. The photograph shows the works on 11 August 1966.

The new fire engines for Pudsey, seen here in 1917, were a great advance on the previous engines, which were pulled by horses. They had to be caught in their paddock on Cemetery Road, which was sometimes a lengthy process, if they were tired after pulling hearses or cabs.

This photograph was presented to Superintendent Dockray by the members of the Pudsey Fire Brigade, on his retirement in 1925. The men and machines are in front of the former fire station, in the Market Place.

## Section Six

# SCHOOLS

*Pupils and teacher pose for a school photograph at Greenside Board School, 1890.*

The solemn faces seem to indicate the length of time these children had to keep still when having their photographs taken at Primrose Hill School, 1898.

An infant class at Richardshaw Lane School, early twentieth century.

A class of Standard IV girls at Littlemoor School, *c.* 1920. The school was started in 1883 in the Sunday school of Littlemoor Wesleyan Chapel. In 1901 the school moved to new premises higher up Valley Road. The building shown is now demolished.

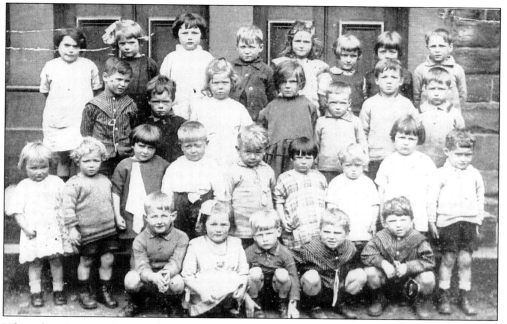

When this photograph was taken in 1920, Mount Tabor School was held in the Sunday school rooms of Mount Tabor Chapel, Waterloo Road.

The new Secondary and Technical School, Richardshaw Lane, opened on 21 January 1911. The girls in the foreground are wearing what was probably the school uniform. The school later became Pudsey Grammar School, and is now a comprehensive named Pudsey Grangefield.

These girls of Pudsey Grammar School seem to be congratulating one another, but the occasion, c. 1930, is not known.

Mrs Main with her class from Waterloo County Primary School, 1956. The group is outside Mount Tabor Sunday School, which was used as an annexe to the school. Mrs Main came to Pudsey from Monymusk, Aberdeenshire, in about 1930.

The staff of Waterloo School, 1947. Mr Gaunt (headmaster) is seated in the middle of the front row, with Miss Jackson and Mr Senior (deputy head) on either side. Also pictured are Miss Robinson, Mrs Main, Miss Mann and Mr Sykes.

Pupils of Priesthorpe School decorated this room for Mrs M. Hamilton, who was eighty-two and partially sighted, in November 1967. They are, left to right, Gina Sutherland, Richard Ramsey, Joan Atkinson, Terry Ball, and John King.

# Section Seven

# WARTIME

*Pudsey men of the Yorkshire Dragoons form a Guard of Honour for*

*King George V in France, 1916.*

Men from the West Yorkshire Regiment, before going to France, 1916. They include Eliot Crowther (back row, second left) and George Frankland (back row, first left).

A Leeds recruiting tram of the First World War. These trams travelled round the Leeds district, including Pudsey, exhorting young men to join up. Martial music was played by a band inside the tram.

Women of the AFS stand in front of their vehicle at Westroyd, Farsley, *c.* 1940. They include E. Dufton, M. Davies, T. Gorman, H. Gargrave and J. Barker.

The air-raid wardens of Pudsey West Post, New Street and South Parade, and include C. Mathers, H. Pickup, A. Jackson, J.L. Gibson and ? Rayner.

Women air-raid wardens of Pudsey old borough, 1940s. Back row, left to right: N. Slater, N. Haigh, Mrs Harper, Mrs Brown, A. Dixon, R. Haigh, A.L. Sugden, R. Shackleton. Front row: -?-, D.M. Slater, Mrs Cooper, N. Turnpenny, -?-, -?-, M. Gambles.

The air-raid wardens of Post PE3, Lowtown, were probably photographed in Verity's Place, Lane End. Post PE3 was situated in ground floor rooms of 120 Lowtown, now The Beauty Parlour. The wardens include W. Jackson, J. Livesey, A. Dalby, L. Hearman, M. Gambles, B.C. Dunton and J. Walker.

Pudsey Town Hall protected with sandbags during the Second World War.

Civil Defence personnel march past the cenotaph to mark the end of the war in 1945.

# Section Eight

# SPECIAL OCCASIONS

*A float, decorated for the coronation of King Edward VII in 1901, stands outside the home of S. Cordingley, owner of Priestley Mill.*

An elaborately dressed group pose outside the front door of Old Hall Farm, Woodhall Hills, after the wedding of Mr Ernest Procter to Miss Emma Walker, 1908. Miss Walker was the daughter of Thomas Patterson Walker and Margaret Walker, and was one of ten children. The bride's numerous family are on the left; Mr Procter is on the far left. Mrs Procter is standing between two seated ladies, Mrs Walker and her daughter Janey.

A carnival carriage at Brunswick Road, 1913. It is outside Spencer's, photographers. Frederick William Walker is holding the horse, with an employee, Lewis Lee, in the carriage with brothers Thomas, George and William Walker.

Mayor James Stillings with the mayoress in his carriage at Greenside, 1902. They are probably going to the carnival. Mrs Stillings presented the mayoral chain to the borough in 1900.

A flower-decked carriage with the carnival queen and attendants, attracts admiring looks as it waits in Greenside, *c.* 1900.

A float waits outside the Liberal Club, Lowtown, to join the procession, 1920s.

Mayor George Womersley is held to ransom by pirates and dusky maidens at the carnival of 1926. Also pictured, in the centre of the photograph, is 'Parky' Wright, who combined the role of park warden with that of mace-bearer for several mayors.

A float from Cliff Mills, 1930. The theme of gold-diggers is taken from a series of popular musicals of the time, which would have been screened in one of Pudsey's two cinemas.

A Remembrance Day service held in the graveyard of Sunfield Wesleyan Methodist Chapel, 1920s.

The Duke and Duchess of York, later to become King George VI and Queen Elizabeth, stand at the door of the St Lawrence Clinic in April 1928. In the background are Nurse Schofield and Dr Squires. The occasion was the official opening of the clinic and children's playground, both of which had been given to the borough by Councillor John B. Ward. During a tightly packed schedule outlined in the souvenir programme, price 3d, the duke laid the foundation stone of the baths with a silver trowel. In the afternoon the playground was opened by the cutting of a ribbon by the duchess, which was the signal for 150 'specially chosen' children to set all the apparatus in motion, while the royal couple walked through the playground to the clinic.

A group pose outside Mount Tabor chapel, before leaving for a trip by charabanc, early 1920s. These vehicles were dual purpose, as the bodies could be taken off and replaced with a lorry body for everyday work.

Robin Lane Primitive Methodist float carries a temperance message. The recreation ground and Hutton Terrace can be seen in the background.

Princess Elizabeth with Mayor D.V. Hodgson on a visit to Pudsey on 27 July 1949, when she was accompanied by the Duke of Edinburgh. They presented a visitors' book for the mayor's parlour, and planted two trees in the children's playground that had been opened by her father twenty-one years earlier.

A bonfire on Greentop built for the coronation of King George V in 1911. The day began with a church service attended by Mayor Walter Forrest. In the afternoon came sports, bands and tea-parties. At dusk the bonfire was lit using 160 gallons of tar and oil, followed by a firework display provided by the mayor.

St George's Day parade of Pudsey Scouts and Cubs, leaving the market square for a service in Pudsey parish church, April 1961.

A group of children enjoy their Christmas party tea, given by the Pudsey Rotary and Round Table, 1958.

Passengers boarding the first aircraft to fly from Yeadon (now Leeds/Bradford) airport to Copenhagen, 1961. Mayor and Mayoress Henry and Mrs Thompson are in the doorway. Others include, left to right, Mr Tom Illingworth (second in from the left), Miss Pudsey Chamber of Trade, Mr and Mrs Reg Milner, Mr and Mrs R. Cruse, Mr and Mrs H. Wilson and Mr and Mrs Wm Crabtree.

Tommy Dick, 1920. He had a wooden hut down Greenside, from which he sold *Sporting Pink* and the *Green Post*.

Dr W.J. Halliday, former head of Pudsey Grammar School, who was a poet and a writer in Yorkshire dialect. For many years he was the secretary of the Yorkshire Dialect Society. The photograph was taken in May 1961.

PC 751 'Bobby' Main came to Pudsey from Stonehaven, Scotland, in the 1930s and remained with Pudsey Police until retirement as Sgt Main in 1960. PC Main is related to the schoolteacher Mrs Main (see pp. 71 and 72), possibly her nephew, although this is not absolutely sure.

Councillor Simeon Myers, far right, selling flags for Pudsey medical charities, at St Lawrence Cricket Club ground, *c.* 1937. H.C. Mann is second from the left.

The annual Mayor's 'At Home' 1964. The mayor (centre) was Douglas Merritt, and the deputy mayor (second left) was George Dunkerley.

This picture of Alderman Sir Walter Ward and Lady Ward was taken on the occasion of his knighthood, in the New Year's Honours List, 8 January 1959. Alderman Sir Ward had already been awarded an OBE for 'services to the wool trade'. He was knighted for 'work done on behalf of fellow citizens'. He was Chairman of the Wool Textile Delegation, a magistrate and a Sunday School Superintendent.

Mayor Douglas Merritt receives nomination papers for the 1964 General Election from candidates T. Wilson (Liberal), Joseph Hiley (Conservative) and Bernard Atha (Labour). Mr Joseph Hiley won.

The crowd of onlookers is gathered for the opening of the Central Sunday School and Institute for Trinity Methodist Church, March 1911. Some of the officials present are Charles Webster (with buttonhole), William Lumby Webster (with white beard), Matthew H. Webster (looking through the railings), and John Hinchcliffe (looking towards the camera). The building is on the site of the former Manor House.

Mr Job Ross of Lowtown receives his chain of office as President of the National Association of Tripe-dressers, from the retiring president, 11 May 1961.

Mr T. Kitchen demonstrates his own invention, the folding car-boot bicycle, 2 May 1963.

Mr Brian Halliday at work, 1962. He was the owner of the flower shop Serendipity at Fulneck End and ran flower arranging courses. His flower arrangements were a feature at many important occasions.

## Section Nine

# FARSLEY

*Town Street, Farsley, c. 1900. The outsize top hat was the trademark of C. Lee and*
*Sons, Merchant Tailors, Hatters, and Costumiers.*

Carts in Walton's Croft. The carts belonged to Farsley UDC when Farsley was a separate Urban District. The site is now the car park of the New Inn, Town Street.

Sandgate, Town Street. This street was built alongside Woodhouse's mill. In the 1861 census it contained nineteen households. The site has now become a car park.

Town Street, Farsley *c.* 1930. Between the shops and the Wesleyan Chapel is the low building housing the fire engine.

Council Offices, Farsley, decorated for the Coronation, 1911. After Farsley UDC amalgamated with Pudsey Borough in 1937, the offices became a library; latterly it has become a dental practice.

Reuben Gaunt, Springfield Mill, was once an important woollen manufacturer employing hundreds of workers. The buildings are now let out to a variety of businesses.

A 57–ton boiler being delivered to Gaunt's Mill, 7 December 1967. Traffic was held up for more than an hour on Bagley Lane.

The weaving department of John Hainsworth & Sons, Cape Mills, was noted for the production of cloth for army uniforms. The shed is decorated here for the 1911 Coronaton.

Hainsworth's dispatch department is sending off a consignment of cloth for Afghanistan, via Liverpool, in 1964.

Farsley Urban District Council, *c.* 1930. The group includes Wilson Haynes, B. Atkinson, M. Overend, Jesse Stephenson, S. Hardisty, B. Cockshott and W.H. Vickers.

The residents of Clara Street show off their finery in the decorated street, for the 1905 carnival. The 'nursing sister' in the centre is a dummy, brought out for each year's carnival.

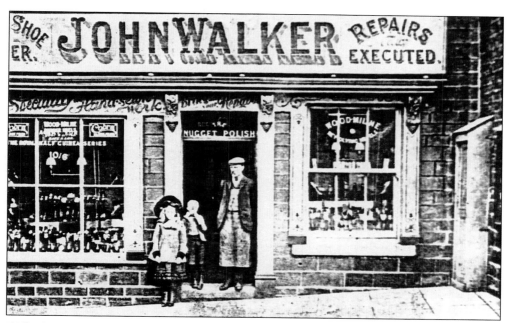

Walker's, Town Street, was one of three boot and shoe manufacturers in the Pudsey area, the other two being Scales and Son, Cemetery Road, and Salter and Salter's, Lane End. Between them they employed hundreds of people. The little girl in the doorway is Miss Walker, who died in 1994, aged 100 years.

Hiram Sutcliffe stands in the doorway of his greengrocer's shop in Town Street, with his son Sydney in his arms, 1921. He began his business with a horse and cart.

Farsley firemen stand beside their engine in Town Street, 1920s. The fire chief is Willie Jeffrey, the driver is Jack Coulter, and the fireman is Joe Fenton.

This well-stocked shop was one of a number owned by the Driver chain in the West Riding area in 1932. Farsley housewives could buy all their requirements in the village, but shopping was a daily chore on foot, not a weekly stock-up at the supermarket.

REV. **SAMUEL MARSDEN,**
BORN FARSLEY, 28TH JULY 1764,
DIED SYDNEY,

The plaque in Farsley Town Street shows Farsley's famous son, the Revd Samuel Marsden. Born in the village in humble circumstances on 28 July 1764, he was apprenticed at an early age to a blacksmith. He studied in his spare time and gained a place at Hull Grammar School. Here he did so well that the Elland Society funded his further studies at Cambridge University. Ordained in 1793, he went as chaplain to the penal colony of Botany Bay, Australia. On one of his visits he brought back to England a sample of the harsh Australian wool, which made up into very coarse cloth. King George III received Marsden, and presented him with six fine Merino sheep from his own flock at Windsor. This was the humble beginning of the lucrative Australian wool trade. Until his death in 1838, Samuel Marsden continued his missionary work in Australia and New Zealand.

The bi-centenary of Marsden's birth occurred in 1964, when Mr G.D.L. White, Deputy Commissioner for New Zealand, planted a tree in the memorial garden, Farsley. He is seen here with the Revd R.E. Marsden, great-great-grandson of Samuel Marsden. The memorial bears the carved likeness of a Merino sheep.

The parish church of St John the Evangelist, Farsley, was consecrated on 27 October 1843 by the Bishop of Ripon. On the north side of the chancel is a tablet which records that the church '. . . was built by subscriptions aided by grants from the Church Building Societies amounting to £1,892 19s 10d obtained through the exertions of the Revd Samuel Redhead, Vicar of Calverley by whom the foundation stone was laid on 8 July 1842.' The vicar certainly had a hard time trying to raise the money. Farsley was a village of poor people, and such of them as went to a service on Sunday preferred the Nonconformists. The villagers only contributed £16 towards the cost. However, the vicar managed to interest some eminent people, and even the Dowager Queen Adelaide. The site for the church, graveyard and vicarage was given by Thomas Thornhill, Lord of the Manor of Calverley, together with a subscription of 100 guineas. The clock was erected in 1853 by William Potts of Leeds, the dials being presented by John Butler, who had them made in his Stanningley foundry.

Farsley Baptist Chapel, Calverley Lane, pictured just before its demolition. It was 100 years old when it was pulled down in 1970. The congregation has now joined with Farsley Methodists to form Farsley Community Church.

Farsley Baptist Chapel (Rehoboth), Bagley. This chapel is part of a long tradition of Baptist ministry in Farsley, stretching back to 1780. In 1869 it was replaced by the building shown above after which it was used as the Baptist's Lower Sunday School for many years. The old Rehoboth chapel is now used as business premises.

Farsley Baptist graveyard contains the graves of the important Gaunt and Hainsworth families. Their elaborate memorials contrast with the plain simple chapel in the previous picture.

Alderman Richard Ogden, chairman of the housing committee, lays the foundation stone of the first house in the Farfield estate, on 21 December 1945, watched by Richard Cruse, town clerk, alderman George P. Jackson and Mrs Jackson, mayor and mayoress, R. Keighley, Mrs Ethel Ogden, Taylor Croft and J. Hill.

Farsley Baptist AFC, 1909. Like most chapels and churches, Farsley Baptists also ran a cricket team in the summer.

An early Guide company in Farsley, with their leader Mrs Moffatt, 1909. The girls are Edna Shaw, Nellie Pearson, Florrie Hart, Fanny Williams, Florrie Sowden, Gertie Shaw, Nellie Gaunt, Marian Allen, Ada Gains, Olive Suddards, Maria Tillotson and Emma Speight.

Farsley Baptist Guides and Brownies welcome the mayor and mayoress, Councillor Gordon Busfield Kitching and Mrs Kitching, to their chapel in 1960, World Refugee Year.

Farsley Cricket Team, 1934. Members include M. Dowgill, Threapleton, Clough, Taylor, Steele, Sutcliffe, A. Dowgill and Hainsworth.

Farsley Celtic AFC were the Yorkshire League champions in 1960. Shown here are R. Hanson (president), Mr Beardon, B. Faulkner, R. Thomas, R. Green, B. Twigg, A. Brown, E. Taylor (trainer), C. Crowley, R. Brown, N. Turton (secretary), C. Horsley (coach), K. Hunt, B. Brown, K. Squire, J. Fowds and B. Peat.

Farsley Celtic AFC were again Yorkshire League champions in 1969, when the players were Bawcombe, Exley, Haxby, Burton, Hardcastle, Hughes, Jones, Senior, Brown (captain), Aveyard and Sanders.

# Section Ten

# CALVERLEY

*An aerial view of Holly Park Mill, 1930s.*

Cottages. These old cottages were not finally cleared until the mid 1930s. The village post office was in a room in one of these cottages, before their demolition in about 1914. The Green was the site of the village well, and was also known as Town Wells.

A group of people set off for a carriage drive, *c.* 1910. They include S. Banks Hollings, D. Hinchcliffe, Ernest Grimshaw, A. Grimshaw Gibbons, Walter Gott and Samuel Parkinson.

St Wilfrid's Church, Calverley, is the mother church of an extensive parish which once included Pudsey, Farsley, Idle, Windhill and Wrose. Until the Marriage Act of 1836, all marriages in this parish had to take place at Calverley. The Norman church has had many later additions and alterations, the last major restoration being in the nineteenth century, but there is evidence of an earlier Saxon foundation. This view of the church was taken from the old vicarage, and shows the church partly obscured by a fine Georgian double house. Built in the early eighteenth century, the house was probably originally owned by the Calverley family, but it later passed into the ownership of the Thornhills. The left-hand portion of the house was a farmhouse, with barn and outbuildings.

Here are some members of Calverley Urban District Council in 1935. Henry Gott (vice-chairman) is in the middle of the back row and S. Banks Hollings is sitting on the far left. Other members of the Council were R. L. Wilde (chairman), Ralph Grimshaw, Fred Outhwaite, H. Calvert, C.A. Pearson, J.M.Waite and C. Pratt. R.S.Haley was the Surveyor, Arthur Davidson the Clerk to the Council and J.E. Thornton the Rating Officer.

Needle Eye, Calverley Cutting, *c.* 1910. This was one of four lodges built as part of a plan to develop Calverley woods as a commuter area, following the advent of the railway linking Leeds and Bradford in 1846. The scheme came to nothing, and the Needle Eye has now been demolished

Boiler house staff Mr F. Hudson and Mr I. Moorhouse take a break at Holly Park Mill, 1939. The mill was opened as a company mill, so that individual manufacturers could rent out portions of it, in 1869. It was closed as a mill in 1972, and now once more is the home of many varied businesses.

The Old Hall, Woodhall Road, was the original home of the Calverley family. The solar (centre) was built in about 1300. The chapel (left) and hall (right) were built in 1485, the porch being a much later addition.

The Thornhill Arms dates from 1673, and until 1880 it was known as the Leopard. When all weddings had to take place at Calverley church, it was much favoured as a refreshment stop before the guests walked back home.

# Section Eleven

# FULNECK

*A family group outside their home in Fulneck village, c. 1900.*

*Unfortunately, their names are not known.*

Fulneck Moravian settlement. The Moravians originally came from Bohemia (Czechoslovakia) whence they fled to Germany because of persecution. The first Moravians sent as ministers to Yorkshire came in the early 1740s. In 1744 22 acres on the south side of Pudsey were bought on which to build a Moravian Settlement, later to be called Fulneck. On 17 April 1780 John Wesley visited Fulneck and noted in his diary that there was 'a chapel, lodging rooms and apartments for Single Sisters and Single Brethren and Widows' as well as a farm and bakery, and also tailoring and cloth making businesses. He did not mention the boys' and girls' schools which had moved to Fulneck in 1753 and 1755 respectively. Originally they were for children of Moravian missionaries and ministers although later fee paying non Moravians were accepted. Eventually the Single Sisters' and Single Brethrens' Houses were incorporated into the schools. The two schools combined in 1994 to become Fulneck School.

The chapel (in the foreground) was consecrated in 1748, the porch and cupola being added a little later. Beyond are the Widows' House and (the larger building) the Single Sisters' House.

The Christian Endeavour Class of Fulneck Sunday School turned out in force for the wedding of their leader, Mr W. Swithenbank, to Miss Langley, in the early twentieth century. The girls in the class include Lily Ramsden, Dora Ramsden, Lily Wilson, Matilda Ogden, Elsie Wilson, Nancy Ogden and Clara Robinson.

Fulneck Moravian Sunday School scholars in their 'Eskimo Village' float. They are in the carnival procession of 1930. A youthful Len Hutton looks on.

A group of cottages at Fulneck. A worker in his leather apron stands outside his workshop. The two cottages in the foreground have now been made into Fulneck Museum.

Miss Louisa Hutton of East Terrace, Fulneck, with Sir Gwilym Williams at the National Savings Headquarters in London. She is receiving the British Empire Medal for her tireless work for the National Savings movement. She is accompanied by her nephew, Sir Len Hutton.

Bankhouse, with well. The walker is coming down from Greentop, traditional site of celebration bonfires. In 1912, when this picture was taken, the well on the right, fed from a spring, was in constant use.

Moravian Church Sunday School children gather with their teachers for a group photograph, *c.* 1910.

# Acknowledgements

For loan of photographs: Donald and Winnie Eke, Pudsey Civic Society Collection, Andrew McDermid.

Information and advice: Ted Garnett, Andrew McDermid, Ruth Strong, Jane Tinker, Mary Tordoff, and members of the public who identified people on the photographs.

Print-making: Jack Calvert.

Books quoted: *History of Pudsey*, Simeon Rayner; *Life and Times of St John's Church, Farsley*, B.H. Bretherick.

Visit our website and discover thousands of other History Press books.

**www.thehistorypress.co.uk**